Cold War Air Combat

Czechoslovak MiG-15 & USAF F-84E

Czechoslovak-West German border Region – 10 March 1953

HUGH HARKINS

ISBN: 1-903630-17-7
ISBN-13: 978-1-903630-17-4

COLD WAR AIR COMBAT
CZECHOSLOVAK MIG-15 & USAF F-84E
CZECHOSLOVAK-WEST GERMAN BORDER REGION – 10
MARCH 1953

© Hugh Harkins 2018

Centurion Publishing

United Kingdom

ISBN 10: 1-903630-17-7
ISBN 13: 978-1-903630-17-4

This volume first published in 2018

This research paper has adopted the Chicago Manual of Style referencing for bibliography and footnotes, although, in some instances, it forgoes shortened repeat notes or the use of *ibid* for the sake of clarity

CONTENTS

ABSTRACT

This research paper details the only documented air combat between North Atlantic Treaty Organisation and European Eastern Bloc jet fighter aircraft during the Cold War. This incident took place near the West German- Czechoslovak border on 10 March 1953 when United States Air Force F-84E fighter aircraft were engaged by Czechoslovak MiG-15 fighter aircraft. This engagement resulted in one of the F-84E's being shot down, climaxing several years of claims and counter claims of airspace violations. The paper attempts to separate fact from non-fact and puts forward answers to the disputed questions of aircraft numbers involved, where the combat was initiated and the reason for the resort to force.

1

COLD WAR AIR COMBAT: CZECHOSLOVAK MIG-15 & USAF F-84E, CZECHOSLOVAK-WEST GERMAN BORDER REGION – 10 MARCH 1953

There was a large number of air incidents between the Soviet Union (and her Eastern European satellite states) and NATO (North Atlantic Treaty Organisation) nations during the first few decades of the period in history defined as the Cold War. The majority of the major incidents, most of which involved the United States and the Soviet Union (USSR – Union of Soviet Socialist Republics), were interceptions by one side or another of mainly transport or reconnaissance/intelligence gathering aircraft, both civil and military.[1] Some of these incidents resulted in aircraft being fired upon, some incidents resulting in aircraft being shot down. However, there were very few incidents that could be classified as air battles involving relatively equal opposing forces. One such incident, however, occurred on the border region of West Germany (Bavaria) and Czechoslovakia on 10 May 1953.[2] The protagonists involved were two Republic F-84E Thunderjet fighter aircraft of the USAFE (United States Air Force Europe) 12th Air Force and two first generation MiG-15 (NATO reporting name 'Fagot') jet fighters of the Czechoslovak Air Force.[3]

Over the ensuing sixty four years various accounts, lacking any great detail, have been presented to favour one side or the other from a legal, political, military or moral standpoint. This paper sets out to present the facts as borne out by official documentation, news reports, personal accounts by those involved,

---

[1] NATO (North Atlantic Treaty Organisation) was a defense treaty entered into by the major western powers on 4 April 1949

[2] Referred to as West Germany, the Federal Republic of Germany was founded in 1949 and covered the French British and American zones of occupation

[3] Czechoslovak MiG-15's received the local designation S-102

geography, details of the relative flights of the aircraft involved and, not least, the political and military situation in the region leading up to the incident.[4] The paper also draws on a number of documents produced before and in the aftermath of the 10 March 1953 incident. The personal papers detailing the incident are both contemporary and produced over five decades later.

The 10 March 1953 air incident was itself the culmination of several years of increased border tensions between the United States and Czechoslovakia, with claim and counter claim of air violations of the Czechoslovak-West German (Bavarian) border by both parties.[5] This included flights by jet fighter aircraft in strengths that could at times be equated to small scale fighter sweeps. In addition, Czechoslovakia registered several protests, as did other East European states and the Soviet Union, claiming that American multi-engine aircraft had penetrated deep into each of the Eastern Bloc nation's airspace on nocturnal biological warfare missions, during the course of which Colorado Beatles were claimed to have been dropped with the aim of destroying crops in the summers of 1950 and 1952.[6]

Only a few years prior to the 10 March 1953 incident the Czechoslovak air force had been considered an ineffective force equipped with an assortment of obsolete World War II aircraft types that were relatively unfit for operational service, including the enforcement of sovereignty of Czechoslovakia air space.[7]

---

[4] Several differing accounts have been presented by the same pilot and USAF departments throwing reasonable doubt on their reliability

[5] The area of West Germany in question, referred to as the US Zone of Responsibility, was administered by the United States under the four power agreement between the Soviet Union, Great Britain, the United States and France – the victorious powers in Europe at the end of World War II

[6] The Soviet note of 30 June 1950 and the Czechoslovak note of 10 July 1950 charged that the aircraft involved were American. A Czechoslovak radio broadcast on 23 June 1952 referred to unidentified nationality aircraft. Department of State Bulletin, 24 July 1950, 134. An East German radio broadcast the same month asserted that American aircraft dropped Colorado Beatles on East German soil. FBIS, Daily Report, 25 June 1952. A Moscow radio broadcast on 19 August 1952 stated that American aircraft had dropped Colorado Beetles on Czechoslovak crops. Trends and Highlights of Moscow Broadcasts, 27 August 1952

[7] Intelligence report 25X1A, prepared as a supplement to intelligence report 25X1X, the former dated 12 April 1951, estimated the Czechoslovak air force at a combat strength of 12 squadrons, unchanged in number from late 1945 levels. The S-90 Czechoslovak variant of the German Me-109 piston engine fighter remained the main fighter with 1 Regiment of 3 squadrons operational in Bohemia and 2 Regiments operational in Moravia. The jet fighter element of the air force consisted of S-91/92's assembled from parts from German Me.262 twin jet fighter aircraft abandoned at the end of World War II and captured by Soviet forces. The 15 or so S-91 (Juno 300

Faced with high performance jet powered fighters of the USAFE 12th Air Force based in southern west Germany, Czechoslovakia began to modernise with MiG-15 jet powered fighters in the early 1950's, units equipped with these aircraft being molded into a more efficient force tasked with protecting Czechoslovak airspace.[8]

At the time of the 10 March 1953 incident the USAFE 12th Air Force, among other types, operated the Republic F-84E Thunderjet jet powered fighter aircraft. Indeed, it was this type of aircraft that was tasked with intercepting aircraft violating the airspace of the United States Zone of Responsibility in West Germany. Despite the superiority of the MiG-15 over the F-84, convincingly demonstrated in the skies of North Korea prior to the 10 March 1953 incident, the type constituted the main aircraft equipment of USAFE Fighter Groups stationed in West Germany in 1953.[9] Contemporary assessments had shown that the F-84E was inferior in most respects to the MiG-15, including maximum speed, and the type suffered in air combat as a result.[10] On the other hand, the rapid firing 0.5 in caliber machine gun armament of the F-84E was considered to be superior to the slow firing 23 mm and 37 mm cannon armament of the MiG-15 (this armament, although having a heavier hitting power was primarily designed for use against slow moving targets such as multi-engine bomber aircraft) in an air combat environment that pitted jet fighter aircraft against jet fighter aircraft.

F-84E's had been deployed to Korea with the SAC (Strategic Air Command) 27th FEW (Fighter Escort Wing) in December 1950.[11] However, with the advent of the MiG-15 in the Korean theatre the F-84E's proved to have insufficient speed to successfully operate against the swept wing Soviet fighter.[12] This inadequacy proved disastrous for an aircraft tasked with the bomber escort role.[13] One

---

jet engines) and S-92 (Juno 400 jet engines) were gathered at Kbely, where training operations commenced in 1949

[8] The Czechoslovak air force began to equip with the MiG-15 in the period circa 1951 (certainly in regards to training in the Soviet Union)

[9] The F-84E entered service with the USAF in 1949. M.S. Knack, *Encyclopedia of USAF Aircraft & Missile Systems, Post World War II Fighters* (Washington D.C: Office of Air Force History, 1978), 33

[10] H. Harkins, *F-84 Thunderjet, Republic Thunder* (United Kingdom: Centurion Publishing, 2013), 43

[11] Knack, *Encyclopedia of USAF Aircraft & Missile Systems,* 1978, 33

[12] The first American aircraft encounters with MiG-15's over Korea occurred in November 1950

[13] Knack, *Encyclopedia of USAF Aircraft & Missile Systems,* 1978, 34

example of the ineffectiveness of the F-84E in the bomber escort role was aptly highlighted during a mission of eight 307th Bomb Group B-29's attacking Namsi Airfield, North Korea on 23 October 1951. On the approach to the target, MiG-15's attacked and evaded interception by the F-84 escort and three B-29's were subsequently shot down. Most of the remaining bombers in the formation were damaged.[14]

As noted above, the 10 March 1953 incident was preceded by more than two years of protest and counter protest over airspace violations on the US Zone of Responsibility German (Bavarian)-Czechoslovak border. The Czechoslovak government had handed a diplomatic note of protest to the US government on 22 January 1951, the contents charging the US with 58 recorded violations of Czechoslovak air space during the period October 1950 [specific date not given] to 15 January 1951.[15] This note has proved elusive, but the contents, reproduced in a Reuters report, charged that the violations were deliberate and with purpose rather than accidental.[16] An English translation of a Radio Prague broadcast on 13 March 1953 stated that eight of these violations of Czechoslovak air space had occurred in October 1950, 18 in November 1950, 6 in December 1950 and 26 in the period of 1 January-15 January 1951.[17]

The political arguments between the US and Czechoslovak governments over alleged airspace violations continued through 1951. One of the more embarrassing incidents for the US occurring on 8 June that year, when a pair of USAFE jet aircraft (F-84) landed in Czechoslovakia.[18] These aircraft were not officially reported missing until 10 June 1951, when searches of NATO controlled territory proved fruitless. On 12 June, the US sought assistance form the Soviet Union in the search for the missing fighter aircraft in her zones of influence in Eastern Europe. On 14 June, the US charged that the aircraft had come down in Czechoslovak territory and that the pilots were being detained by Czechoslovak authorities. This charge was pushed forward in a US government statement issued on the 15th. The following day the Czechoslovak government reply confirmed that it had detained two USAF pilots and their aircraft while it investigated the circumstances of the violation of its airspace. Following a series of diplomatic

[14] Harkins, *F-84 Thunderjet*, 43. Some operational documents give the date for this raid as 23 October, while others point to the raid having taken place on 25 October, the former considered the more accurate

[15] A.L. George, *U.S. Air Force Project Rand Research Memorandum, Case Studies of Actual and Alleged Overflights, 1930-1953* - Supplement(s), RM-1349, (California: The Rand Corporation, 15 August 1955), 118

[16] Reuters report carried in the New York Times, 23 January 1951, and reproduced in George, *Actual and Alleged Overflights, 1930-1953*, 122

[17] George, *Actual and Alleged Overflights, 1930-1953*, 119

[18] George, *Actual and Alleged Overflights, 1930-1953*, 123-124

exchanges, in which the US sought to convince the Czechoslovak government that the violation of its airspace had been unintentional pilot error during a training mission, the Czechoslovak government agreed to return one of the pilots to the United States, but indicated that it would return the other pilot to Norway as he was a Norwegian citizen and had requested same.

On 22 June 1951, two weeks after the 8 June incident, the Czechoslovak government charged the US with no less than 116 violations of its airspace since 15 January that year.[19] One of these incidents occurred on 7 February 1951 when two USAFE fighter jets (F-84) crossed the border from West Germany into Czechoslovakia and flew almost to Prague.[20] The Czechoslovak government protested this violation on 9 February, this being met with blank denial from the US Embassy in Prague. On the 17th of February, the US admitted the charge of the violation of Czechoslovak airspace and presented an apology to the Czechoslovak Foreign Office.[21] The diplomatic note of apology, or admission of culpability, included a reassurance that USAF high speed aircraft (inferred as jet powered combat aircraft) were not to fly within ten miles of the Czechoslovak border.[22]

Another Czechoslovak diplomatic note protesting air violations was handed to the US government on 24 July 1952, citing the 'intentional violation' of Czechoslovak air space by West German based aircraft of the USAF.[23] Further diplomatic exchanges between the Czechoslovak and US governments charged the latter with continued violations of the formers airspace during the period June, July and August 1952. The major point of these notes was that 'notwithstanding assurances to the contrary from the United States government', violations of Czechoslovak airspace by US aircraft had continued at the same rate as prior to the assurances being given in February 1951.[24]

On 21 November 1952, the Czechoslovak government issued a formal warning

---

[19] This charge was reported in a Washington dispatch to the Washington Post on 26 June 1951, for inclusion in the 27 June 1951 issue. George, *Actual and Alleged Overflights, 1930-1953*, 118-119

[20] The Czechoslovak capital was circa 110 km (just under 70 miles) miles from the West German frontier

[21] This statement intimated that the two American aircraft had 'inadvertently crossed the border of the U.S. zone [Germany] with Czechoslovakia on February 7, when they became lost on a training mission, and, mistaking the Prague beacon for the Mammendorf beacon [West Germany], flew to the vicinity of Prague'. George, *Actual and Alleged Overflights, 1930-1953*, 122

[22] The diplomatic note stated 'that crews of the United States Air Force flying high-speed aircraft are under standing orders not to go within ten miles of the Czechoslovak border'. George, *Actual and Alleged Overflights, 1930-1953*, 122

[23] George, *Actual and Alleged Overflights, 1930-1953*, 202

[24] George, *Actual and Alleged Overflights*, 1930-1953, 202

to the US government that if the violations of its airspace continued then action would be taken to force the offending aircraft to land or they would be shot down.[25] This warning was issued in a climate of increased Czechoslovak assertiveness of the defence of her airspace, made possible by the introduction of high performance fighter aircraft in the shape of the MiG-15. This more assertive stance included shadow operations in which Czechoslovak fighter aircraft would be sent up to conduct parallel flights on the Czechoslovak side of the Czechoslovakia-West German border as a counter to American fighter aircraft patrols on the West German side of the border.[26]

The accusations of airspace violations were not all one way traffic, there being several reported incidents of Czechoslovak aircraft overflying villages on the West German side of the border with Czechoslovakia. One such incident was reported by West German (Bavarian) Border Police as having occurred on 4 March 1952.[27] Further reports of West German airspace violations by Czechoslovak aircraft were reported by West German (Bavarian) Border Police on 7 July 1952. This report charged that there had been five overflights by Czechoslovak jet powered aircraft over the course of the previous week (presumably 1-7 July).[28] The West German Border Police issued a statement to the effect that these aircraft had overflown the Bavarian villages of Zwiesel, and Wolfstein, a few miles on the West German side.[29] West German Border Police further reported that Czechoslovak aircraft had crossed the border into Bavaria several times during the course of February 1953.[30]

That a potential clash between USAFE F-84E jet fighters and Czechoslovak MiG-15 jet fighters was a growing possibility appeared to be obvious, certainly for the historian looking back on events of 64 years prior. However, at the time it

---

[25] Office of Current Intelligence, Current Intelligence Bulletin, Document No.57, 11 March 1953, 4

[26] Office of Current Intelligence, Current Intelligence Bulletin, Document No.57, 11 March 1953, 4

[27] This incident was reported to have involved two MiG's, presumably MiG-15's, bearing Czechoslovak markings, which, the report claimed, flew over the town of Weiden in the U.S. administered zone of West Germany, some 12 miles from Czechoslovakia-West German border. The incident was not mentioned by US authorities until 6 June 1952. There must be a degree of ambiguity in the West German Border Police reports as the aircraft would have presumably have been flying at altitudes in excess of 10,000 ft., rendering visual identification very difficult at best

[28] George, *Actual and Alleged Overflights, 1930-1953*, 217

[29] The New York Times, 8 July 1952. This may be Wolfenstein which lies about 10 km from the Czech border, Zwiesel lying less than 5 km from the border

[30] George, *Actual and Alleged Overflights, 1930-1953*, 218

may well have looked like the diplomatic game of protest and counter protest would continue indefinitely without escalation into armed conflict, even of an ephemeral nature. However, when taken in the context of the large number of air incidents in other areas of the West Europe-East Europe border zones, it seems clear that tensions on the West German (Bavarian)-Czechoslovak border were, in 1951-1953, higher than on those other border zones. One reason for this may well have been the fact that the vast majority of air violations that were vehemently protested were of the nature of high speed jet fighter aircraft, on both sides, as opposed to say the Berlin Air Corridors, where most violations that were protested were conducted by slow moving multi-engine aircraft. There were of course occasions when NATO aircraft were fired on and, on occasion, shot down in the Berlin air corridor. It is a point of fact that there were more incidents of aircraft being fired on in zones such as the Berlin air corridor, however, these were seen in a similar light to other incidences of multi-engine, piston and jet powered, aircraft being shot down by Soviet aircraft on authorised transits or intelligence gathering missions in various zones and not in the light of two sides provoking each other on opposing sides of a land border as appeared to be the case with USAFE and the Czechoslovak air force in the border areas of West German (Bavaria) and Czechoslovakia.

The actual and alleged border violations over the previous two and a half years or so had passed off without either side resorting to force. In early March 1953, the atmosphere of the early Cold War period was thrown into uncertainty by the death of the Soviet Premier Joseph Stalin.[31] Eastern Bloc defences were on alert to counter any potential NATO attempts to make capital of the changeover of power in the East, perhaps by a series of border violations that may or may not have been designed to portray the Eastern Bloc as weakened under its new leadership.[32] It cannot be determined to what extent this affected air defence policy in Czechoslovakia at that time, but, with tensions already high through years of air violations, the stage seemed set for the armed confrontation between Czechoslovak and American aircraft, which took place on the morning of 10 March 1953 when two Czechoslovak MiG-15 jet fighter aircraft engaged two American F-84E Thunderjet jet fighters, one of the latter being shot down.

On 11 March, the day after the air battle, the Czechoslovak government issued the US government with a diplomatic note in which it was stated that the two American aircraft had crossed into Czechoslovak airspace and continued their penetration to a depth '18 kilometers [~11 miles] south southwest [of the Czechoslovak town] of Plzen [Pilsen]) at a distance of around 40 km from the state frontier'.[33] The note continued, 'At this point the Czechoslovak fighters [two

---

[31] Stalin passed away on 5 March 1953

[32] There were a number of incidents in the Berlin Air Corridor at this time, including the shooting down of a RAF Avro Lincoln bomber on 11 March, either slightly inside East German airspace or, as is disputed, over West Germany, wreckage falling on both sides of the frontier

MiG-15's] intercepted the American aircraft and issued signaled instructions for them to land'.[34] The note of protest went on to state that the Czechoslovak pilots request to land was ignored and that 'In the air battle [resulted from the American aircraft attempting to escape] one of the U.S. aircraft fled in a westerly direction, the second was hit and, steadily losing altitude, disappeared in a southwesterly direction'.[35] The Czechoslovak government handed another diplomatic note to the US government on 28 March 1953, in which it pressed that its version of 11 March was accurate, adding 'the previously mentioned facts are based on the logbook records of the land radio mechanics, the goniometer records, and the radar reports, as well as on the statements of the Czechoslovak pilots'.[36]

Five decades after the incident the Czechoslovak pilot that had shot down the F-84E, Colonel Jaroslav Sramek, recalled the air engagement for Radio Praha, in which he recounted the following text:

'I spied a pair of planes, which were not ours. They were F-84s. They were clearly encroaching on our airspace. I reported the situation and I received orders to fire a warning shot. There was no other possibility of apprehending them. I was to detain them and get them to listen to my instructions. Unfortunately, it didn't turn out like that. We were the ones who saw them first, which is always a tactical advantage. But then they saw us immediately afterwards. Straight away they tried to evade us. They banked sharply and flew off at full throttle. But because the MiG 15's were better [than] the F-84's we were able to turn easily and manoeuvre into a position where we could fire a warning shot. The warning shot hit his backup tank on the right hand side. Fuel started escaping from it. He tried to escape to the south. In view of the fact that I was higher than him I was able to catch him easily and my second round disabled him. After firing the shot I saw flames coming from his craft so I stopped and headed home'.[37]

While the Czechoslovak version of events, if lacking important details such as the altitude the engagement was initiated at, remained constant in the months that followed the incident. The same, however, certainly could not be said for the US government versions(s) of events that changed several times. In fact, the Czechoslovak version and the American version even differed in regards to meteorological conditions at the time of the engagement. The Czechoslovak

[33] FBIS, Daily Report, March 12, 1953

[34] FBIS, Daily Report, March 12, 1953

[35] FBIS, Daily Report, March 12, 1953

[36] Department of State Bulletin for 10 August 1953, 183

[37] 'Czech Fighter Pilot Recalls Cold War Dogfight', 04.10.2004, Radio Praha broadcast, http://www.radio.cz/en/section/curraffs/czech-fighter-pilot-recalls-cold-war-dogfight

version indicating conditions of poor visibility while the American pilot that was shot down, in an interview for Life Magazine, indicated that visibility was good.[38]

On the day of the incident a document was produced by the US Office of Current Intelligence Indications Staff carrying the following text: 'The US 12th Air Force reports that MiG-15 aircraft attacked two USAF F-84 jet fighters at 10008Z, 10 March 1953. One F-84 was shot down, the other landed safely'.[39] The document continued to state the position that the F-84E that was shot down had crashed at as '49° 05' N, 12° 25' E, about 22 nautical miles from the Czech [Czechoslovak] border near Cham, US Zone Germany'. The document also confirmed that the second F-84E had escaped from the MiG-15's and subsequently landed at the USAFE airfield of Füerstenfeldbruck, near Munich.[40]

The initial US version of events unambiguously stated that the F-84E's were on a routine patrol.[41] The F-84E pilot debrief report stated that 'The US aircraft were attacked at 49° 15'N, 120° 25'E, about 16 nautical miles from the Czech [Czechoslovakia] border inside the US zone [of Germany]. The debrief document continued that 'The F-84 pilots sighted MIG-15's about 3,000 feet above them, circled to investigate, and thereupon found MIG-15's on their tails'.[42] The debrief document went on to state that one of the F-84 pilots claimed two MiG-15's were involved while the other stated, erroneously, that five MiG-15's were involved.[43]

On the afternoon or evening following the incident, USAF intelligence put forward two hypothesis as to the reason for the action taken by the Czechoslovak pilots. Both of these hypothesis assumed that the engagement had taken place over Bavaria. The first of these reasons seemed the only probable one (from an American standpoint), in that the Czechoslovak pilots actions were the result of observing US aircraft (number undetermined, but assumed to be the two F-84E's) on a heading that would have indicated an intention by the US pilots to overfly Czechoslovak airspace.[44] In the days following the incident US ground based radar plots confirmed that there was a violation of Czechoslovak airspace by a US aircraft (type undetermined) at 0826Z, just over one and a half hours prior to the combat between the MiG-15's and the F-84E's.[45] This being the case, then it

---

[38] Life Magazine, Vol. 34, No.12, 23 March 1953, 30

[39] Office of Current Intelligence Indications Staff, 10 March 1953

[40] Office of Current Intelligence, 10 March 1953

[41] Office of Current Intelligence, 10 March 1953

[42] Office of Current Intelligence, 10 March 1953

[43] Office of Current Intelligence, 10 March 1953

[44] Office of Current Intelligence, 10 March 1953

[45] Untitled USAF Intelligence document NSA25X dated 16 March 1953, 2

would seem logical for Czechoslovak air defences to be on alert for further intrusions. If the aircraft noted above to be on a heading that indicated a possible intention to overfly Czechoslovak airspace was in reference to one or both F-84E's then it can be inferred that USAF intelligence accepted they were on a heading toward Czechoslovak airspace, although this was refuted in a release dated 16 March, in which it was claimed that the F-84E's were 'flying northwest on a heading of 320° at the time of the attack'.[46] If such a heading is accepted and, if the Czechoslovak version of events is considered the more plausible, then the F-84E's would indeed still have been on a heading that would deepen their penetration into Czechoslovak airspace. The second of the USAF speculations regarding the reason behind the Czechoslovak action was a retaliatory action (presumably acting under Soviet orders) for the defection of a Polish Air Force MiG-15 (piloted by a Polish national).[47] This hypothesis can be discounted and is included here only for posterity.

On 16 March 1953, the USAF released further information on the incident to the effect that the F-84E that had been shot down had crashed at reference point 49° 05'N, 120° 25'E, near the town of Cham, in West Germany, a distance of some 22 miles from the Czechoslovak frontier.[48] The F-84's, it was stated, had 'sighted MIG-15's about 3,000 feet above them, circled to investigate, and thereupon found the MIG-15's on their tails'.[49] This indicated the MiG-15's were flying at an altitude of around 15,000 ft. as a later statement by the F-84E pilots to the media stated they themselves were flying at an altitude of 13,000 ft.[50] The 16 March release changed the US version of events in the context that the F-84E's were no longer claimed to have been on a routine patrol, but were now in fact claimed to have been specifically ordered into the air to 'intercept unidentified aircraft near the Czech [Czechoslovak] border'.[51]

In an interview for Life Magazine, the pilot of the F-84E that was shot down, Lieutenant Warren G. Brown, stated that the F-84E's had taken off from the USAFE airbase at Fursty (Füerstenfeldbruck) at 10.45 am on 10 March 1953. He indicated that he was flying at 13,000 feet, above and behind the lead aircraft flown by the other F-84 pilot, Lieutenant Donald C. Smith.[52] When the two F-

[46] Untitled USAF Intelligence document NSA25X dated 16 March 1953, 2. This may well be in reference to another aircraft

[47] Office of Current Intelligence Indications Staff, 10 March 1953

[48] Untitled USAF Intelligence document NSA25X dated 16 March 1953, 1

[49] Untitled USAF Intelligence document NSA25X dated 16 March 1953, 1-2

[50] Life Magazine, Vol. 34, No.12, 23 March 1953, 30

[51] Untitled USAF Intelligence document NSA25X sated 16 March 1953, 1

[52] Life Magazine, Vol. 34, No.12, 23 March 1953, 30

84E's were around 7 or 8 miles from the Czechoslovak frontier they then altered course to a heading of 360° in a North East direction. At or around this point, Brown states that he saw 'two silvery specks about a mile ahead', to which he called out a warning to Smith. Almost immediately one of the MiG-15's dived toward Smith, apparently passing over his aircraft. Brown then states that the MiG veered to the left and he followed after them, continuing to turn at which point he lost Smith. He then states at this point he looked over his shoulder and noted a MiG-15 on his tail and he continued to tighten up his turn in the course of three complete 360° circuits, but the MiG stayed on his tail, closing to under 1,000 feet. At this point Brown states that the MiG-15 on his tail opened fire, the F-84E being hit and flipping over on to its back, but the aircraft continued to be controllable, allowing him to retrieve it from the dive it was now in. His overheat light showing and notable damage to the starboard stabilizer, Brown set course for Füerstenfeldbruck (having requested a heading from Smith), at which point his starboard tip tank fell away from the aircraft. This was probably shot away in the second attack of which it appears that Brown was oblivious, Smith stating that he observed the MiG-15 closing for a second attack and open fire.[53] This is also confirmed by the statement of the Czechoslovak pilot.[54] Following the second attack (following the loss of the starboard wingtip fuel tank) Brown states that the aircraft started 'vibrating violently' and continued that the 'right wing suddenly opened up' and debris and smoke and, or, vapour, came through the hole.[55] The aircraft appearing to be doomed, Brown ejected.

It can, with a reasonable degree of confidence, be concluded that available evidence supports the Czechoslovak contention that only two MiG-15's were involved in the incident. This is borne out by the fact that the statements of the American pilot who was shot down and the Czechoslovak pilot of the MiG-15 that shot the F-84 down, together with the indelible fact that the statements of involvement of additional MiG-15's carried in a hastily prepared Intelligence Report on 10 March was added to 17 Months after the incident with assertions that MiG-15's from other nations (presumably East European or the Soviet Union) were also involved.[56] The pilot of the F-84E that was shot down stated that he did not know what happened to the second MiG-15 during the engagement, but assumed he had lost interest in the F-84E's. He then goes on to state 'I still had my own MiG... to worry about.[57] His statement at no point

[53] Life Magazine, Vol. 34, No.12, 23 March 1953, 30

[54] 'Czech Fighter Pilot Recalls Cold War Dogfight', 04.10.2004, Radio Praha broadcast, http://www.radio.cz/en/section/curraffs/czech-fighter-pilot-recalls-cold-war-dogfight

[55] Life Magazine, Vol. 34, No.12, 23 March 1953, 30

[56] This claim first appeared in a US communication a considerable time after the incident

[57] Life Magazine, Vol. 34, No.12, 23 March 1953, 30

mentioned any MiG-15's other that the two observed at the commencement of the encounter.

What remains a point of contention is the location that the initial encounter actually took place – Czechoslovak or West German airspace, although it can be concluded that the encounter certainly ended on West German territory if we determine the crash of the F-84E as the end of the incident. The Czechoslovak pilot was convinced that the shots fired at the F-84 were fired on the Czechoslovak side of the border and that the trajectory that the stricken American aircraft was on at the time of the fatal impact would have carried it across the border to the point of crash some 35 km (22 miles) on the West German side of the border.[58]

One point of note that would point to Czechoslovak airspace being the initiation location is that there is no USAF report that indicates the scrambling of further USAF fighter aircraft to support the F-84E's, which would certainly have been expected to happen in the event that combat aircraft of a foreign power intruded in West German airspace and attacked USAFE aircraft, an attack that lasted no less than six or seven minutes in duration. While this does not prove beyond contestation that the encounter was initiated over Czechoslovak airspace it does provide food for thought for the historian. Another point is that the F-84E pilots did not drop their external fuel tanks in their endeavour to escape the MiG-15's, standard practice for an aircraft involved in air combat. One potential reason for this, assuming an initiation of combat in Czechoslovak airspace, may have been that to drop the tanks over Czechoslovakia would have been tantamount to an admission of a violation of that nation's sovereign airspace with the added punch of endangering the population on the ground. It would, of course, be deemed more desirable to escape without leaving physical evidence of an intrusion. The pilot of the F-84E that was shot down stated that he did not drop his auxiliary tanks because he did not "think he'd [the MiG-15 pilot] shoot at me over the U.S. Zone".[59] However, even after the attack had commenced Brown failed to drop his auxiliary tanks.

The distance from Plzen (Pilsen) in Czechoslovakia (the area where the Czechoslovak pilot statement states the F-84E's were intercepted) to Cham in West Germany (the area where the F-84E piloted by Brown crashed) is just over 90 km (56 miles).[60] The maximum speed of an F-8E was around 521 nautical mph (~599 mph).[61] Even assuming a lower speed of 580 mph, with simple

[58] The F-84E that was shot down was last observed by the Czechoslovak MiG-15 pilot to be on a South Easterly heading. Reported in FBIS, Daily Report, March 12, 1953

[59] Life Magazine, Vol. 34, No.12, 23 March 1953, 30

[60] To this must be deducted 11 miles or so as this is the distance to the south southwest of Pilsen that the American aircraft are stated to have been intercepted

[61] Knack, *Encyclopedia of USAF Aircraft & Missile Systems*, 1978, 50

mathematics it becomes clear that it is entirely possible that close on 70 miles could have been covered in the seven minutes from the attack being initiated until the F-84E crashed. In light of this fact it cannot be determined that an incident was initiated over West German airspace simply because the F-84E crashed on West German territory. The above values do not take into account a deduction of the ~11 miles to the south southwest of Pilsen that the F-84E's were reported to have been intercepted or factor in combat maneuvering of the F-84E in the attempts to evade being shot down or a deduction of. However, even when dividing the straight line distance value flown by half, there remains sufficient distance covered to leave open the question of whether the interception took place over Czechoslovak or West German territory. This is due to the fact, which has to be taken into consideration, that an aircraft flying at 13,000 ft. altitude (the stated height of the F-84E's at the time of interception), even if it disintegrated in the air, which it did not, would, due to its considerable forward momentum bestowed by a flight speed in excess of 550+ mph, travel a considerable distance before impacting the ground. Assuming an intact plane in a more gradual descent while under power, then it would not be unusual for several tens of miles to be covered. The fact that the pilot landed by parachute on the German side of the border after ejecting from the stricken F-84E cannot in itself be considered indisputable evidence that the incident was initiated over West German territory. It should be remembered that the Czechoslovak pilot broke off the attack and turned away before the F-84E (last observed on a south westerly heading) pilot ejected from the aircraft, so there is only one version as to how soon after the attack that the pilot abandoned the aircraft. Even Browns version of events would leave little doubt that this was no less than several minutes after the MiG-15 opened fire. The Czechoslovak contention obviously being that the aircraft travelled some distance toward, and perhaps across the Czechoslovak-West German border prior to the pilot ejecting.

Some press and diplomatic coverage from the 1950's expressed the view that neither of the American pilots had made it clear as to why they had not returned fire against the Czechoslovak MiG-15's.[62] While there was certainly a lack of detail in regards to Smith from the American side, the same cannot be regarded as true for Brown. It was clear from his interview in Life Magazine that Brown was, at no time during the incident, in a position in which he could bring his guns to bear.[63] The USAF department in Washington D.C. confirmed that it was of the opinion that the F-84E's lacked the necessary speed to be able to maneuver into a firing position against the faster MiG-15's.[64] This was apparently echoed by a USAF spokesperson at a press conference in the German town of Wiesbaden to the effect that the F-84 pilots had not had the opportunity to return fire.[65] At this

[62] George, *Actual and Alleged Overflights, 1930-1953*, 257

[63] Life Magazine, Vol. 34, No.12, 23 March 1953, 30

[64] Washington Evening Star, 11 March 1953

press conference the obvious was revealed when the USAFE spokesperson stated that American pilots on the type of patrol that the F-84E's were on, at the time of the incident, were 'told to avoid all possible trouble when encountering strange aircraft', but that they were under standing orders to 'fight back if attacked with a clearly hostile act or if it is a matter of saving life'.[66]

The Czechoslovak pilot interview was quite clear as to why neither of the American pilots had returned fire – this being due to a tail chase nature of the engagement as the Czechoslovak MiG-15(s) pursued the F-84(s).[67] A Rand report published in 1955 goes on to assert that the American pilots and USAFE spokespersons failed to make clear why defensive action was not taken. Again, Brown had made it clear that he was trying to evade the MiG-15, clear defensive action.[68] The Czechoslovak MiG-15 pilot also made it clear that the American aircraft tried to evade the MiG-15 attack by banking sharply and flying away at full throttle, as did the Czechoslovak government diplomatic notes of protest.[69] In the American diplomatic note of 18 August 1954, what seemed like an incredible claim was made to the effect that the American pilots had not returned fire as the guns on their aircraft had been rendered inoperative. While all pertinent information has to be taken into account, this latter claim should certainly be taken in context that it did not appear until more than seventeen months after the incident and should, therefore, be considered in the context of the diplomatic battle that was still ensuing – the US attempting to portray the American pilots as innocent victims of an aggressive act by the Czechoslovak pilots under orders to affect the destruction of American aircraft purely for political capital.

On 14 March 1953, a USAFE spokesperson, speaking in Wiesbaden, confirmed that American pilots conducting patrols on the West German-Czechoslovak border had received orders 'not to give an inch' and would, therefore, unlike the British 2nd Tactical Air Force, continue flight operations right up to the border with Eastern Bloc countries.[70] A mere 5 days later, on 19 March, USAFE confirmed that its pilots had now been ordered not to fly within 30 miles of the West German border with Czechoslovakia or East Germany, except when ordered to do so on flights aimed at intercepting air intruders, or, when flying through air corridors that were recognised by the Soviet Union.[71] The same

[65] George, *Actual and Alleged Overflights, 1930-1953*, 257

[66] George, *Actual and Alleged Overflights, 1930-1953*, 257

[67] 'Czech fighter pilot recalls cold-war dogfight', 04.10.2004

[68] Life Magazine, Vol. 34, No.12, 23 March 1953, 30

[69] 'Czech fighter pilot recalls cold-war dogfight', 04.10.2004

[70] The British 2nd Tactical Air Force stationed in Northern West Germany was under instructions not to fly closer than 10 miles from the East German border during routine flying

communique stated that such an air policy had actually been in effect since the previous year, giving the face saving impression that US policy had not been altered by the 10 March incident.

Whether or not US policy had changed in regard to air operations near the West German borders with her East European neighbours, policy on the ground (air) appeared to have changed, leading to a somewhat easing of tensions. There still remained protestations of provocative overflights from the Czechoslovak government, but these were in response to unidentified nocturnal flights by multi-engine transport type aircraft and the release of balloons carrying propaganda leaflets. The period of stand-off between groups of high speed combat aircraft was over, the 10 March 1953 incident passing into history as the only fighter versus fighter combat of the Cold War era in the European theatre.

Figure 1. Map showing the modern day border between Germany and the Czech Republic, which remains representative of the 1943 West Germany-Czechoslovakia border in regards to the western border with Germany. ©2018 GeoBasis-DE/BKG/2009 Google

---

[71] George, *Actual and Alleged Overflights, 1930-1953*, 260

Figure 2. Modern map showing the German-Czech Republic (representative of 1953 West German-Czechoslovak) border and extended area covering the German towns of Munich and Nuremberg and the Czech towns of Prague and Pilsen. ©2018 GeoBasis-DE/BKG/2009 Google

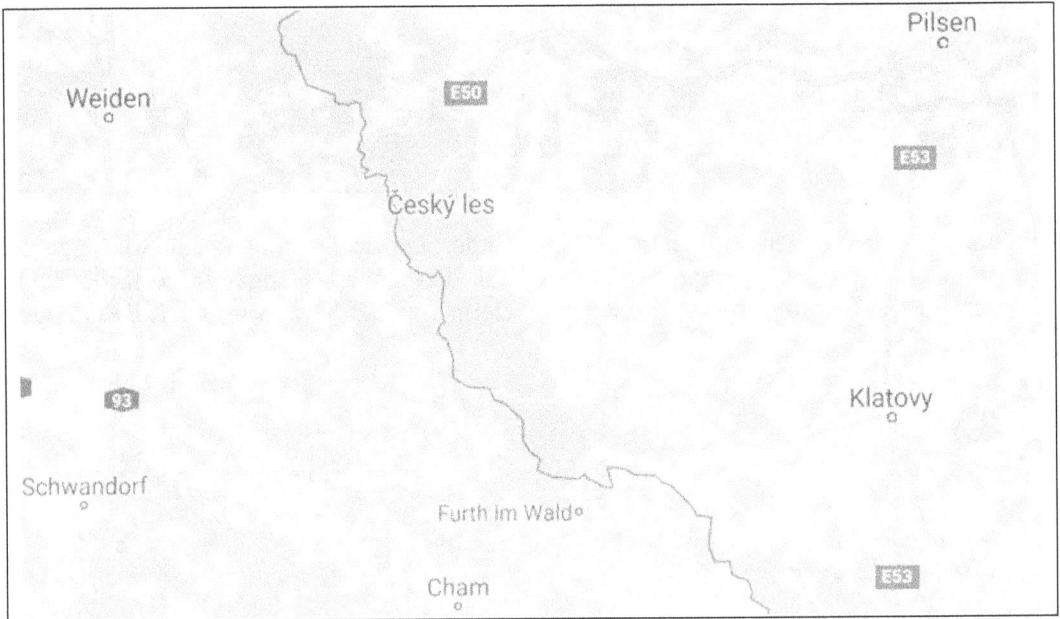

Figure 3. Modern day map showing Cham (lower centre), in modern day Germany, located ~22 nautical miles from the Czech Republic [1953 Czechoslovak] border. Pilsen (shown at upper right) is located somewhat over 90 km (56 miles) to the north east of Cham. ©2018 GeoBasis-DE/BKG/2009 Google

ADDENDUM I

Republic F-84E Thunderjet - The F-84 emerged from studies that resulted in a General Operational Requirement issued on 11 September 1944. This specified a day fighter featuring mid-set wings and performance that included a top speed of 600 mph and an armament of either 8 x 0.50 calibre or 6 x 0.60 calibre machine guns (later being reduced to 6 x 0.50 or guns). On 12 March 1945, a definitive contract was signed for three aircraft designated XP-84 (powered by a single J35 (licence built de Havilland Goblin) turbojet engine). The design suffered development problems leading to a modified design being introduced in July 1945, the third XP-84 being built to XP-84A standard. Additional XP-84A's were built, followed by 226 production P-84B, 181 F-84C, 154 F-84D and 843 F-84E's. The major production variant however was the F-84G (improvement of the F-84D).

It was the F-84E that equipped the 12th Air Force in March 1953. This variant, which emerged on 29 December 1948 when the F-84 program underwent an overhaul, was powered by the J35-A-17 turbojet engine. Changes introduced included a lengthened fuselage, stronger wing, more spacious cockpit, a radar gun sight (initially an A-1B was specified, but this was replaced by the A-1C) and improvements to the fuel system, which included the wingtip fuel tanks and provision for 230 US Gallon tanks under the wings, increasing the aircrafts combat radius to more than 1,000 miles.

The first production F-84E conducted its maiden flight on 18 May 1949 and was, along with another aircraft, accepted on the 26th of that month, but full scale deliveries did not commence until 1950. The F-84E served with the USAF until 1956, the US Air Force Reserve relinquished its last F-84E's in 1957 and the type were retired from Air National Guard service in 1959.

F-84E – data furnished by USAF

Engines: One Allison J35-A-17 turbojet rated at 2223 kg (4,900-lb.) thrust
Length: 11.7 m (38 ft. 6 inch)
Height: 3.8 m (12 ft. 7 inch)
Wingspan: 11.1 m (36 ft. 5 inch)
Weights: 6954 kg (15,227 lb.) fully loaded
Maximum speed: 965 km/h (599.5 mph; 521 nautical miles per hour)
Cruising speed: 782 km/h (485 mph)
Service ceiling: 13180 m (43,240 ft.)
Range: 2391 km (1,485 miles)
Armament: 6 x 0.50 in (12.7 mm) caliber machine guns; four in upper nose and 2 inch wings. Maximum bomb load, 907 kg (2000 lb.)

Table 1. General specification values for the Republic F-84E Thunderjet fighter

Figure 4. The XP-84 prototype. USAF

Figure 5. Prior to encountering Czechoslovak MiG-15's over central Europe, F-84 variants had been deployed to Korean in support of United States air operations against Communist forces during the Korean War (1950-53). These deployments had shown the type to be inferior in most respects to the swept wing MiG-15, particularly when the latter was flown by Soviet pilots. Here a quartet of 74th Fighter Bomber Wing F-84's are en route to a communist target north of the 38th parallel. USAF

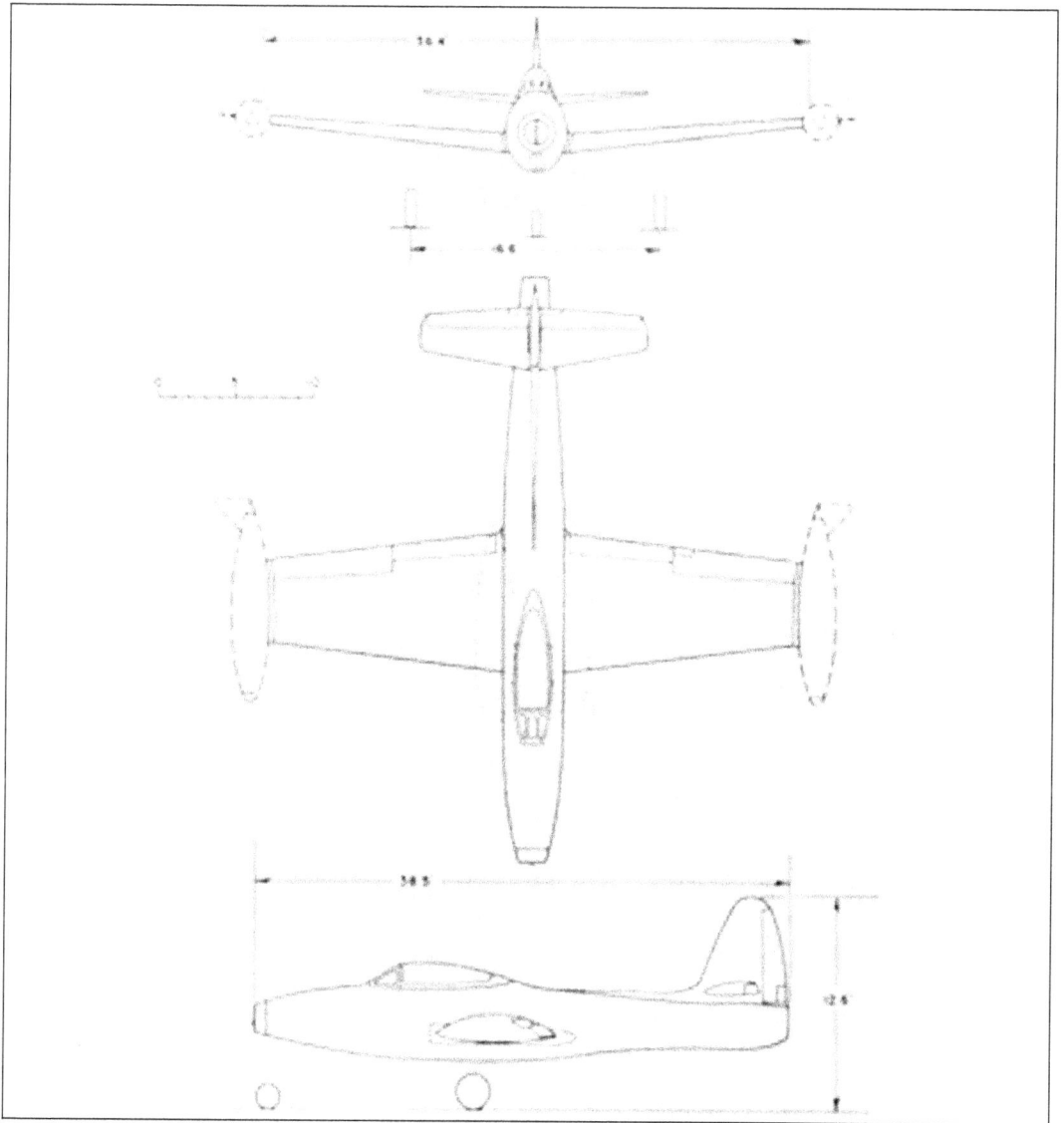

Figure 6. Basic three view general arrangement drawing of the Republic F-84E Thunderjet fighter with wingtip mounted fuel tanks and underwing/fuselage external fuel tanks outlined in broken dashes. USAF

Figure 7. Republic F-84E S/N: 49-2028 of the Wright Field Test Division with wingtip mounted fuel tanks. USAF

Figure 8. F-84E cockpit. USAF

Figure 9. F-84E. USAF

Figure 10. F-84E. USAF

Figure 11. The F-84E, the first of which conducted its maiden flight on 18 May 1949, introduced a number of changes, including a lengthened fuselage. USAF

Figure 12. Top: Eight Air National Guard F-8E's. USAF

ADENDUM II

Mikoyan MiG-15 'Fagot' - Building on jet fighter design experience gained with the MiG-9 that first flew in 1946, the Mikoyan Design Bureau MiG-15 prototype conducted its maiden flight in December 1947 and entered service with the Soviet Air Force in 1949. The MiG-15 was the most promising of the early Soviet post-war jet fighter developments, being powered by the RD-45, a Soviet produced derivative of the British Rolls Royce Nene jet engine. The initial MiG-15 variant was augmented from 1950 by the improved MiG-15Bis that was powered by the VK-1 engine.

Once sufficient numbers had been introduced to service with Soviet air armies and allied states fighting against the US and her allies in Korea, the MiG-15 was introduced to Soviet satellite states from circa 1951-52 – Czechoslovakia receiving operational aircraft in this period, pilots having initially trained in the Soviet Union.

MiG-15Bis

Engine: Klimov VK-1 turbojet rated at 6,000 lb. thrust (early MiG-15's were powered by the RD-45 engine)
Wingspan: ~10.1 m (33 ft. 1.5 inch)
Length: ~10.18 m (33 ft. 3 5/8 inch)
Height: 3.4 m (11 ft. 2 inch)
Maximum weight: 5112 kg (11,270 lb.)
Maximum speed: 1078 km/h (670 mph)
Range: 805 km (500 miles)
Ceiling: 15545 m (51,000 ft.)
Armament: 2 x 23 mm cannon and 1 x 37 mm cannon

Table 2. General specification values for the MiG-15Bis

Figure 13. A MiG-15S of the Soviet Air Force circa 1950's. MODRF

Figure 14. The MiG-15 prototype conducted its maiden flight in 1947. RAC

Figure 15. The MiG-15Bis was an improved variant of the original MiG-15. KnAAZ

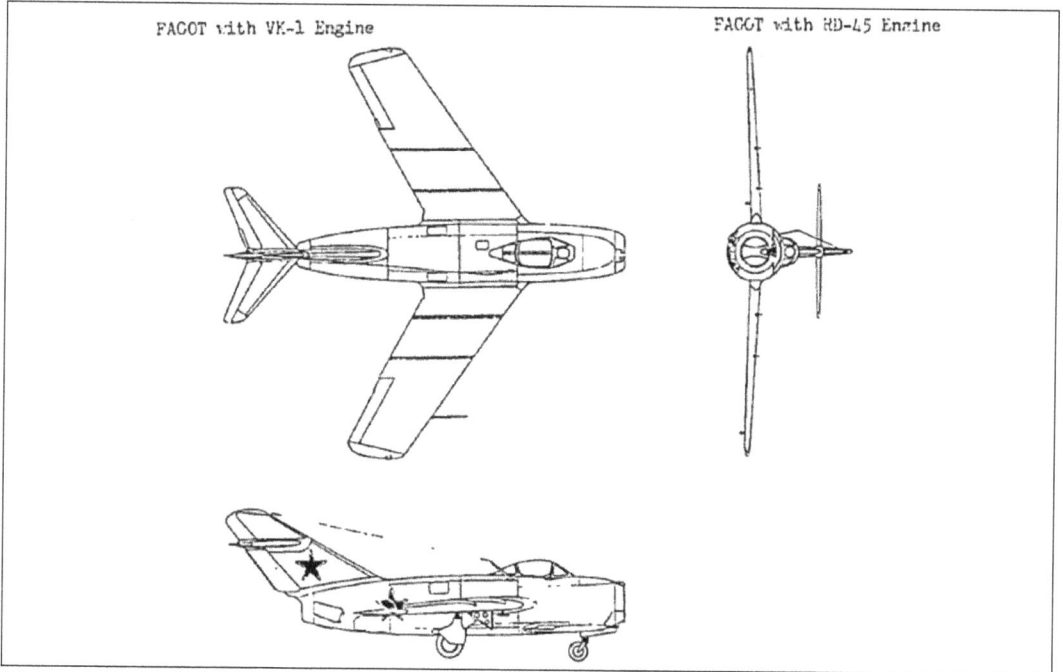

Figure 16. Three view general arrangement drawing of the Mikoyan MiG-15 'Fagot' jet powered fighter. ONI

Figure 17. Cockpit of a MiG15bis jet fighter. USAF

Figure 18. Nose air intake that fed air to the VK-1 engine on the MiG-15Bis. USAF

Figure 19. North Korean MiG-15Bis. This aircraft was flown to South Korea in September 1953 by a defecting North Korean pilot. USAF

Figure 20. North Korean MiG-15Bis in the National Museum of the USAF ay Wright Patterson Air Force Base, Ohio. USAF

Figure 21. The MiG-15 was armed with two 23 mm cannon and a single 37 mm cannon. KB Tochmash

Figure 22. The cannon armament of the MiG-15/Bis was more suited to destroying or damaging slow moving multi-engine bomber aircraft as opposed to high speed jet powered fighter aircraft like the F-84, although the type achieved considerable success in the latter field.

BIBLIOGRAPHY

George, A.L. *U.S. Air Force Project Rand Research Memorandum, Case Studies of Actual and Alleged Overflights, 1930-1953 - Supplement(s), RM-1349,* California: The Rand Corporation, 15 August 1955

Harkins, Hugh, '*F-84 Thunderjet, Republic Thunder*, United Kingdom: Centurion Publishing, 2013

Knack, M.S *Encyclopedia of USAF Aircraft & Missile System, Post World War II Fighters*', Washington D.C.: Office of Air Force History, 1978

'Czech Fighter Pilot Recalls Cold War Dogfight', 04.10.2004, Radio Praha audio broadcast, http://www.radio.cz/en/section/curraffs/czech-fighter-pilot-recalls cold-war dogfight

FBIS, Daily Reports, March 12, 1953

Department of State Bulletin, August 10, 1953,183

Associated Press Interview with the US pilots (published in the Washington Evening Star, March 11, 1953)

Account of the incident by the pilot who was shot down, Lt. Warren G. Brown, Life magazine, Volume 34, No.12, March 23, 1953

Texts of notes of exchange, Department of State Bulletin, March 30, 1953; August 30, 1954

Bonn (Donnelly) to Secretary of State, No.2347, November 21, 1952, citing cable received by USAFEUR from U.S. Air attaché on November 18 (SC 5311); CONFIDENTAIAL

FBIS, Daily Report, March 17, 1953

RM-1348, 'Intelligence Value of Soviet Notes on Air Incidents, 1950-1953' (CONFIDENTIAL)

Reported Interception of US Aircraft over Germany, Office of Current Intelligence Indications Staff, 10 March 1953

Interception of US Aircraft over Germany, Untitled Intelligence Document, March 16, 1953

Office of Current Intelligence, Current Intelligence Bulletin, Document No.57, 11 March 1953

Trend and Highlights of Moscow Broadcasts, 27 August 1952

The New York Times, March 12, 1953

The New York Times, March 17, 1953

The New York Times, May 17, 1953

The Washington Post, March 11, 1953

(Washington) Evening Star, March 11, 1953

(Washington) Evening Star, March 13, 1953

Characteristics and Performance Handbook U.S.S.R. Aircraft, Assistant Chief of Staff/Intelligence-and Office of Naval Intelligence-USN

GLOSSARY

F	Fighter
FBIS	Foreign Broadcast Information Service
FEW	Fighter Escort Wing
ft.	Feet (unit of measurement)
km	Kilometres
km/h	Kilometres per hour
KnAAZ	Sukhoi Aviation Holding Company, Y.A. Gagarin KnAAZ Branch Office
lb.	Pound (unit of weight)
m	Metre
MiG	Mikoyan
MODRF	Ministry of Defence of the Russian Federation
mph	Miles per hour
NATO	North Atlantic Treaty Organisation
ONI	Office of Naval Intelligence
P	Pursuit
RAC	Russian Aircraft Corporation
RAF	Royal Air Force
SAC	Strategic Air Command
S/N	Serial number
US	United States
USAF	United States Air Force
USAFE	United States Air Force in Europe
XP	Experimental Pursuit
~	Approximately equal to (can also be used to mean asymptotically equal)

ABOUT THE AUTHOR

Hugh Harkins, FRAS is a historian and author with an extensive background in astro/geophysics and studies/research in the wider scientific, aeronautic, astronautic and nautical technical and historical fields. Hugh has published in excess of sixty books; non-fiction and fiction, writing under his given name as well as utilising several pseudonyms. He has also written for several international magazines, whilst his work has been used as reference for many other projects ranging from the aviation industry, international news corporations and film media to encyclopaedias, museum exhibits and the computer gaming industry. Hugh is a member of the Institute of Physics and is an elected Fellow of the Royal Astronomical Society. He currently resides in his native Scotland.

Other titles by the author include
Iskander - Mobile Tactical Aero-Ballistic/Cruise Missile Complex
Orbital/Fractional Orbit Bombardment System - The Soviet Globalnaya Raketa
Counter-Space Defence Co-Orbital Satellite Fighter
Sukhoi T-50/PAK FA - Russia's 5th Generation 'Stealth' Fighter
Sukhoi Su-35S 'Flanker' E - Russia's 4++ Generation Super-Manoeuvrability Fighter
Sukhoi Su-34 'Fullback'
Sukhoi Su-30MKK/MK2/M2 - Russo Kitashiy Striker from Amur
MiG-35/D 'Fulcrum' F – Towards the Fifth Generation
Air War over Syria, Tu-160, Tu-95MS & Tu-22M3 - Cruise Missile and Bombing Strikes on Syria, November 2015-February 2016
Sukhoi Su-27SM(3)/SKM
Russian/Soviet Aircraft Carrier & Carrier Aviation Design & Evolution Volume 1 - Seaplane Carriers, Project 71/72, Graf Zeppelin, Project 1123 ASW Cruiser & Project 1143-1143.4 Heavy Aircraft Carrying Cruiser
Light Battle Cruisers and the Second Battle of Heligoland Bight
British Battlecruisers of World War 1 - Operational Log, July 1914-June 1915
Eurofighter Typhoon - Storm over Europe
Tornado F.2/F.3 Air Defence Variant
Air to Air Missile Directory
North American F-108 Rapier - Mach 3 Interceptor
Convair YB-60 - Fort Worth Overcast
Boeing X-36 Tailless Agility Flight Research Aircraft
X-32 - The Boeing Joint Strike Fighter
X-35 - Progenitor to the F-35 Lightning II
X-45 Uninhabited Combat Air Vehicle
Into The Cauldron - The Lancaster MK.I Daylight Raid on Augsburg
Hurricane IIB Combat Log - 151 Wing RAF, North Russia 1941
RAF Meteor Jet Fighters in World War II, an Operational Log
Typhoon IA/B Combat Log - Operation Jubilee, August 1942
Defiant MK.I Combat Log - Fighter Command, May-September 1940
Blenheim MK.IF Combat Log - Fighter Command Day Fighter Sweeps/Night Interceptions, September 1939 - June 1940
Tomahawk I/II Combat Log - European Theatre, 1941-42
Fortress MK.I Combat Log - Bomber Command High Altitude Bombing Operations, July-September 1941
XF-92 - Convairs Arrow

www.ingramcontent.com/pod-product-compliance
Lightning Source LLC
Chambersburg PA
CBHW081251040426
42452CB00015B/2793